# An Album of the American Cowboy

# An Album of the
# AMERICAN COWBOY

by John Williams Malone

illustrated with photographs

Franklin Watts, Inc.
845 Third Avenue
New York, N.Y. 10022

SBN: 531-01512-2
Copyright © 1971 by Franklin Watts, Inc.
Library of Congress Catalog Card Number: 79-151886
Printed in the United States of America

# Contents

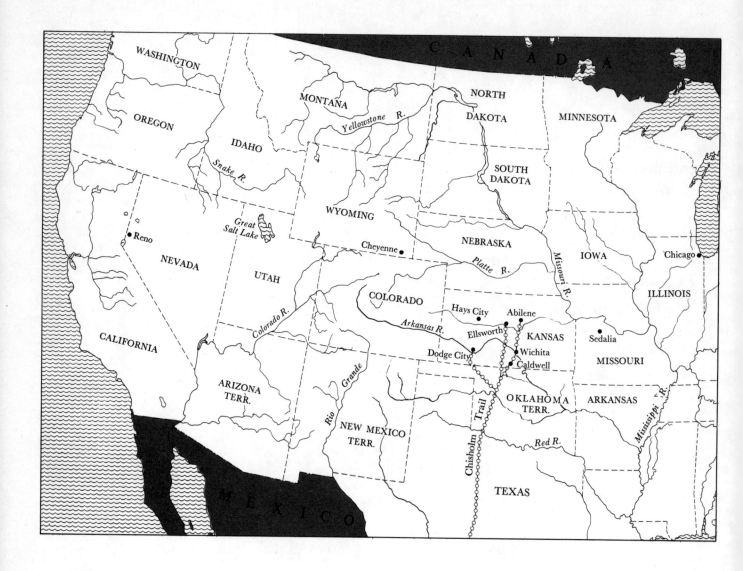

# Introduction

A cowboy is a man who herds and tends cattle. Men have performed the tasks of the cowboy for centuries. But the American cowboy of the late nineteenth century became a figure of special significance. The stories told about the cowboys of that time are legendary. In those years the raising of beef cattle on the vast grassy plains of the West became a great American industry. The cattle were shipped from the West by railroad to packing houses farther east. To get the cattle from the ranches where they were raised to the nearest railroad, the cowboys herded them thousands of miles over the plains. As the railroad tracks were laid farther and farther through the West, new towns sprang up beside them. One town after another became famous as a shipping center for cattle, and as a place of entertainment for the colorful cowboys who tended the herds. And out of these towns came the tales that made a legend of the American cowboy.

# Chapter 1:
# Cattle and Men

Cattle were not native to North or South America. They were first brought to the New World from Spain in the sixteenth century. Spanish explorers had both horses and long-horned black cattle with them on their gold-hunting expeditions in North, Central, and South America. Some of the cattle wandered off and began to run together in wild herds. The descendants of these Spanish Longhorn cattle would become the foundation of the beef industry in Texas and the American Southwest in the last third of the nineteenth century.

*A drawing of a Longhorn by Charles de Granville, a French naturalist who traveled on the western plains of North America in the seventeenth century. His drawings are the earliest-known pictures of American cattle.* (FROM Trail Driving Days, COURTESY OF THE AUTHORS, DEE BROWN AND MARTIN F. SCHMITT)

Cattle ranching in the New World first developed in Mexico. The Mexican cowboys were called *vaqueros*. Vaquero is a Spanish word meaning cow-keeper or cow-herder. Many of the Spanish and Mexican ways of working and dressing were taken over by the American cowboy of the nineteenth century. The American cowboy also used many Spanish words. He called the wooden enclosures in which cattle or horses were kept by the Spanish name *corral*. The ropes he used to capture animals that were running free he called *lassos*. The Spanish word *rancho* became ranch.

*A well-dressed vaquero
on horseback,
by Frederic Remington.*
(NEW YORK PUBLIC LIBRARY)

3

*A vaquero tending cattle, by Frederic Remington.* (NEW YORK PUBLIC LIBRARY)

*The American cowboy took over many of the vaquero's ways of dressing and working.* (THE BETTMANN ARCHIVE)

*Texas cattle crossing a stream.* (THE BETTMANN ARCHIVE)

About the middle of the nineteenth century, cattle ranching
in the American Southwest began to grow in importance.
Before that time, ranchers used their cattle primarily to
feed and clothe their own families; extra meat and hides
were sold in nearby towns. On the open range, or grasslands, lived many herds of wild cattle. Ranchers began
rounding up the wild cattle when they discovered that
their hides, horns, hoofs, and tallow (fat) could be sold in
the North for use in several new manufacturing processes.
But there was still no market for beef.

5

*The cattle market in Chicago, Illinois, 1868.* (THE BETTMANN ARCHIVE)

Between 1861 and 1865, ranching was interrupted by the Civil War. During that time, a man named Philip Danforth Armour made a fortune selling pork to the Union Army. When the war was over, Armour invested his wealth in a meat-packing plant in Chicago, Illinois. A new demand for beef developed in the North. By 1866, a head of Texas cattle could be sold in the North for as much as forty dollars in United States currency. Texas ranchers began to raise beef cattle in greater and greater numbers for shipment to the northern markets.

Men came from many backgrounds to work as cowboys on the growing cattle ranches of the Southwest. Some had served in the Union Army, even more in the Confederate Army. There were young men from the East looking for adventure, and older men who wanted to start a new life. Cowboys did not care very much where a man came from or what he had done before. The cowboy was an independent kind of man, who regularly moved on to new towns and other ranches. The beef industry was getting bigger every day, and there were seldom enough good cowhands to go around.

*Men came from many places to work as cowboys.* (DENVER PUBLIC LIBRARY WESTERN COLLECTION)

*"One Horse Charley" with Shoshone Indians in Reno, Nevada.*
(DENVER PUBLIC LIBRARY WESTERN COLLECTION)

There were many black cowboys working in the Southwest and later in the Northwest. Many ex-slaves, freed by the defeat of the Confederacy, went to work as cowboys. Other black cowboys were freemen who had grown up in the North. Negro cowboys did not experience as much discrimination as did black men in other areas of American society at that time. A number of black cowboys became famous in the West. Isom Dart, Nat Love, "One Horse Charley," and Ben Hodges were among the best-known black cowboys.

Isom Dart was thought by some to be the best horseback rider in all of the West. Like many famous Western figures, he was in trouble with the law for part of his life. (DENVER PUBLIC LIBRARY WESTERN COLLECTION)

Ben Hodges, photographed in Dodge City, where he spent much of his life. (WILLIAM LOREN KATZ COLLECTION)

# Chapter 2:
# The Working Life
# of the Cowboy

Much of the cowboy's work was centered on the roundup. During a roundup, all the cattle belonging to a rancher were gathered together in one place. In the early days of the beef industry, herds of cattle were allowed to graze untended in the grassy open country, called range land. Sometimes several ranch owners joined together in an association. They grazed their cattle on the same range. Each rancher marked his cattle in a different way, so he could tell which animals belonged to him. The marks on the cattle were called brands.

*The beginning of a roundup, by Frederic Remington.* (NEW YORK PUBLIC LIBRARY)

*Looking for cattle
on rough range land,
by Frederic Remington.*
(NEW YORK PUBLIC LIBRARY)

There were two chief reasons for holding a roundup. One
reason was to find all the calves that had been born since
the last roundup, and to mark them with the rancher's
brand. The other was to select the mature cattle that would
be sold that year. During an association roundup, several
groups of cowboys worked on different parts of the range at
the same time. Each group usually included a few cowboys
from each ranch belonging to the association. If all the
cattle belonged to a single owner, the camp was moved to a
different part of the range every day.

The Roundup, *a painting by Charles M. Russell.* (MONTANA HISTORI-
CAL SOCIETY — MACKAY COLLECTION)

*Cutting out a calf.* (THE BETTMANN ARCHIVE)

*If he was trying to cut out a calf, the cowboy went after the mother.*
*The calf would follow her out of the herd and could then be roped.*

After the cattle had been gathered together, the next job was
to separate out the calves to be branded or the mature
cattle to be sold. The job of separating one animal from
the rest of the herd was called "cutting out." It required
more skill than any of the other cowboy tasks. While he was
cutting out cattle from the herd, the cowboy usually rode
a specially trained horse that could stop and turn more
quickly than ordinary horses.

The cowboy had to know how to throw a rope very accurately. Taking his coiled lasso in his hands, he let out enough rope to make a suitably wide noose. Then he twirled the noose in the air above his head to give the rope speed. He aimed the noose for the animal's head and shoulders, or in some cases for its forefeet.

*Steers being roped.* (NEW YORK PUBLIC LIBRARY)

*Branding calves in the nineteenth century.* (OKLAHOMA HISTORICAL SOCIETY)

The custom of branding cattle and horses goes back to the Spanish explorers. In the early cattle-raising days in the American West, the brands were very simple. The end of an iron rod was twisted into the shape of a rancher's initials. A cowboy heated the iron in a fire and then placed it against the animal's hide for a moment, burning the initials into it. Later, ranch brands were made much more complicated, in order to prevent cattle thieves, usually called rustlers, from changing them.

15

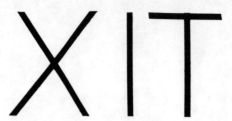

The XIT Ranch

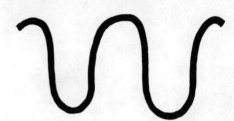

The Running W Ranch owned
by Richard King

The Scissors Brand

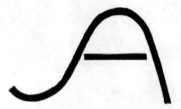

The JA Ranch, owned by
Charles Goodnight and John
Adair

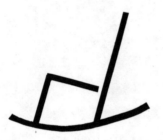

The Rocking Chair Brand

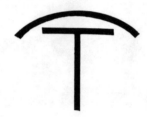

The Quarter Circle T Brand

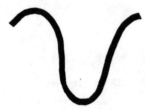

The Flying V of the Matador
Ranch

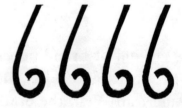

The Four Sixes Brand

*Famous ranch brands of the Southwest. With a hot iron it was easy for rustlers to change a C into an O, or an E into a B. So ranchers began using much more complicated brands that were harder to change.*

Branding was very rough work. After a calf had been roped and dragged to the corral, two or more cowboys held the animal down while the brand was applied by still another man. As soon as a calf had been branded, it was allowed to join the herd again. In northern states, such as Wyoming and Montana, calves were often branded beside a bonfire on the open range. But in Texas a law required all branding to be done inside a corral. Anyone seen branding cattle by an open fire was assumed to be a cattle thief.

*Branding on the 89 Alliot Ranch.* (DENVER PUBLIC LIBRARY WESTERN COLLECTION)

17

One of the most dangerous cowboy tasks was breaking, or taming, horses. It took special talents to break a horse that had never been saddled before. Some cowboys were so good at breaking horses that they did nothing else. They traveled from ranch to ranch all year round. Usually they were paid a fee for each horse they managed to break. The men who specialized in breaking horses were known as bronco busters. Bronco is a Spanish word meaning wild horse.

*A bucking bronco,*
*by Frederic Remington.*
(NEW YORK PUBLIC LIBRARY)

*A typical cowboy horse, by Frederic Remington.* (NEW YORK PUBLIC LIBRARY)

Most of the horses the cowboys rode had been foaled by a tame mare and then allowed to grow up wild on the open range. Some horses were truly wild, the descendants of animals brought to the New World by the Spaniards. The horses that the Spaniards brought were tame, but occasionally one or two of them ran away. These escaped horses banded together into herds which greatly increased in size and number over the centuries. In Texas such horses were called mustangs. In Wyoming and Utah they were called cayuses. But cowboys usually just called them broncos.

A Lowdown Trick
*by William R. Leigh*,
GRAND CENTRAL ART GALLERIES,
NEW YORK CITY)

*Crooked, Any Way You Take him*
*by William R. Leigh.*
(GRAND ART GALLERIES,
NEW YORK CITY)

*Bronco busters saddling a horse, by Frederic Remington.* (NEW YORK PUBLIC LIBRARY)

Many broncos were never completely tamed, and for as long as they lived they would occasionally kick their heels, rear up, and throw their riders into the dust. One reason why broncos were difficult to control was that they were often broken by extremely cruel methods. Later, as the beef industry grew larger, and greater numbers of horses were needed, bronco busters began to treat the animals more humanely. They learned that patience as well as firmness was necessary to train a horse properly.

*The Rope Corral, by Frederic Remington.* (NEW YORK PUBLIC LIBRARY)

A roundup was very hard on horses. Each cowboy often used three or four fresh animals during a day's work at roundup time. When one horse tired, the cowboy headed back to the rope corral where the horses were kept during the day. There he picked out a fresh one. The best horses were usually saved to use at night or during a storm. Ordinarily, a herd of cattle settled down quietly during the night. But if a large herd was gathered in one place, there was always the chance of a stampede. In a stampede, every cowboy wanted to have his best horse under him.

22

Longhorn cattle were particularly nervous animals. It took very little to start a stampede of Longhorns. A distant animal cry or some other chance noise, for instance, might startle one animal from its sleep. If it got up and began to run, the rest of the herd often followed, almost instantly. In a few moments, the entire herd would become infected by blind panic, and a thousand head of cattle would charge off toward the horizon, bellowing and tossing their horns.

*In a stampede,*
*by Frederic Remington.*
(THE BETTMANN ARCHIVE)

A terrified herd of galloping cattle was a sight that filled any cowboy with terror, too. The job of the cowboys on watch was to try to stop the stampede just as quickly as possible. One way to stop a stampede was to ride out in front of the maddened herd, yelling and shooting a pistol into the air in order to start the cattle running in a circle. If a cowboy's horse slipped while he was riding in front of the herd, it often meant the end of the cowboy's life. At best, he was likely to suffer cuts, bruises, and broken bones.

*A cowboy falls in front of a stampeding herd.* (THE BETTMANN ARCHIVE)

*Cowboys trying to head off a stampede.* (DENVER PUBLIC LIBRARY WESTERN COLLECTION)

During a stampede the herd sometimes charged off in the direction of a ravine or cliff, making it too dangerous for cowboys to ride in front of the cattle. On a stormy night, with thunder and lightning, every cowboy had to spend the entire night in the saddle, patrolling the frightened herd to keep it from stampeding. A bad stampede sometimes ended with the loss of more than a thousand head of cattle.

25

*A midnight storm and stampede.* (NEW YORK PUBLIC LIBRARY, RARE BOOK DIVISION)

*A cowboy funeral.* (DENVER PUBLIC LIBRARY WESTERN COLLECTION)

*A bunkhouse in Texas.* (NEW YORK PUBLIC LIBRARY)

Many cowboys were killed in stampedes. If a man was thrown by a bronco, he could easily break his leg — or even his neck. In some parts of the West, cowboys occasionally had to fight off Indians, or shoot it out with rustlers. Yet, in spite of all his hard work and all the dangers he faced, the cowboy was paid only about one dollar a day. In addition, he was given his food, and there was a bunk bed for him to sleep in when he was within riding distance of his home ranch. At most ranches all the cowboys' beds were crowded together in one big room, called a bunkhouse.

27

Often a group of cowboys was too far from the home ranch to return to it at night. Sometimes they could spend the night at a hut on the outlying range. If there was no hut, the chuck wagon became the closest thing to home. At the rear of every chuck wagon was a large storage compartment divided up into drawers and cubbyholes, in which both food and utensils were stored. The cowboys' bedrolls and extra clothing were stored in the front part of the wagon. A canvas cover on iron hoops protected the interior of the wagon in bad weather.

*Cowboys eating from a chuck wagon.* (DENVER PUBLIC LIBRARY WESTERN COLLECTION)

*Cowboys camping at a hut on the outlying range, by Frederic Remington.* (NEW YORK PUBLIC LIBRARY)

*The ranch of Charles Goodnight, who invented the chuck wagon in 1866.* (NEW YORK PUBLIC LIBRARY, RARE BOOK DIVISION)

*Cowboys eating in front of two chuck wagons on the northern plains. Tents were commonly used in the Northwest where the weather was colder, but they were not often seen in the Southwest.* (DENVER PUBLIC LIBRARY WESTERN COLLECTION)

The legend that says cowboys ate nothing but canned beans is untrue. There were usually other kinds of canned vegetables available, as well as canned fruit. Meat, of course, was plentiful. On a roundup or trail drive, cattle were cut out of the herd and killed as they were needed for food. Weak animals or nervous ones that might start a stampede were killed first. Meals also usually included freshly made biscuits, baked over an open fire in a heavy iron pot called a dutch oven. Finally, there was plenty of coffee, tea, syrup, and sugar.

To the visitor from the East, the cowboy's way of dressing seemed colorful and showy. But, in fact, it was sensible and simple. He wore the best kind of clothing for the sort of job he did. His spurred boots, for example, were natural footwear for a man who spent as much as twelve hours a day in the saddle. The high heels on the boots kept the cowboy's feet from pushing through the stirrups.

*A cowboy often spent twelve hours a day in the saddle. A wash drawing by Frederic Remington.* (THE BETTMANN ARCHIVE)

*A nineteenth-century cowboy in typical dress.* (THE BETTMANN ARCHIVE)

The rest of the cowboy's costume was as practical as his boots. The leather chaps he wore over his trousers protected his legs from the underbrush in rough country. His big hat with its wide brim protected him from both wind and rain. These hats were sometimes called by the Spanish word *sombrero*. They were also called Stetson hats, after the manufacturer. The bandana worn around the neck by the cowboy was used for everything from a handkerchief to a bandage to a sling for carrying things in.

Except for an occasional dance in town, the cowboys' forms of entertainment were as simple as the rest of his life. If the men were not too tired, they would sit around the campfire for a while at the end of the day, telling one another tall stories or singing cowboy songs. Most cowboy songs sounded alike. They were often about the loneliness of work on the open range, and they usually had very similar, mournful tunes. Sad tunes had a soothing effect on cattle and made them easier to control. For that reason, the cowboy often sang aloud as he worked.

*Cowboys often sang about the loneliness of work on the range.*

Cowboys sometimes entertained themselves by playing cards, throwing dice or playing mumblety-peg. Mumblety-peg was a game in which several men threw knives into the ground, trying to get them to stand up straight. The cowboys sometimes gambled on these games, but many ranch owners would not allow any gambling among the men except when they were on their own in town. Even when gambling was allowed, the cowboys often gambled for matches instead of money. On trail drives, for instance, few men carried any money with them, and they were not paid until the end of the drive.

*Cowboys gambling.* (DENVER PUBLIC LIBRARY WESTERN COLLECTION)

*A cowboy race, the simplest form of riding contest.* (DENVER PUBLIC LIBRARY WESTERN COLLECTION)

When they did have free time, cowboys sometimes challenged one another to riding contests. Not every cowboy owned his own horse, but each man usually had a favorite among the horses belonging to the ranch. If a man did own his own horse, he often took great pride in the animal's abilities — especially if it was a wild mustang that he had caught and broken himself. Sometimes a group of cowboys took turns trying to ride an unbroken horse. The winner was the man who managed to stay on the longest.

*A drawing of a cowboy horserace that appeared in a German newspaper. The people of foreign countries were fascinated by the American West.* (THE BETTMANN ARCHIVE)

*A cowboy riding bareback on a young steer.* (THE BETTMANN ARCHIVE)

*A cowboy picking a coin up off the ground.* (NEW YORK PUBLIC LI-BRARY)

On special occasions, like the end of a roundup or trail drive, organized riding and roping contests were held. There were a wide variety of events to compete in at these contests. A cowboy could try to ride a bronco or to pick up a coin off the ground while galloping by at top speed. There were roping contests in which the cowboys used the same skills they worked with when cutting out cattle during the roundup. There were contests to determine who could ride the back of a young steer the longest before being thrown. Out of such contests grew the modern rodeo show.

# Chapter 3:
# The Trail Drive

The first large-scale effort at moving cattle for long distances over the Western trails came in 1866. That year many Texas ranchers decided to drive their cattle to the nearest railhead for shipment to the new packing plants in the North. In 1866, the railhead nearest Texas was at Sedalia, Missouri. Along the way to Sedalia, however, many cattle were killed in floods and stampedes. In eastern Kansas, the cattlemen encountered another kind of problem. Kansas farmers were afraid that the great herds of cattle would trample their crops.

*Railroad tracks being laid across the plains of Kansas. The farthest point that the tracks reached was called a railhead.* (KANSAS STATE HISTORICAL SOCIETY, TOPEKA)

*Jayhawkers beating a Texas rancher.* (NEW YORK PUBLIC LIBRARY, RARE BOOK DIVISION)

The farmers had another reason to fear the Texan cattle. In those days, Texan cattle were carriers of cattle fever. The disease did not affect the Texas longhorns; they had been exposed to it for so long that they had become immune. But the farmers' milk cattle were very susceptible to cattle fever. The farmers, who were called jayhawkers, threatened to beat or shoot any cattlemen found crossing their land. So the cattlemen couldn't get through to Sedalia, after all, and had to sell off their herds for very little money.

*Cattle being loaded on railroad cars at Abilene.* (THE BETTMANN ARCHIVE)

In spite of the problems of 1866, the ranchers started to drive their cattle over the trails again in 1867. This time, though, they had a new destination. A man named Joseph McCoy had bought land in Abilene, Kansas, and was developing the small town for cattle shipping. It was far enough west of Sedalia to be out of farming country. Most important, it was a railhead. McCoy built a shipping yard, an office and a hotel, and was ready for business. Word spread quickly that cattle could be shipped through the town. More than 36,000 head of cattle were loaded aboard railway cars at Abilene that year.

40

*Colonel O. W. Wheeler's herd on the trail to Abilene in 1867.* (NEW YORK PUBLIC LIBRARY, RARE BOOK DIVISION)

*Abilene became a boom town, the first of many that were to spring up around the Kansas railheads over the next few years.* (NEW YORK PUBLIC LIBRARY, RARE BOOK DIVISION)

The herds traveled from Texas to Abilene over the Chisholm Trail. The trail was named for a part-Indian trader named Jesse Chisholm, who had first marked out the route several years earlier. It passed through Indian territory, and occasionally a group of cattle traders were attacked. But most Indians were content to charge a toll, usually ten cents for each head of cattle, before allowing the herds to cross their lands. The Chisholm Trail itself went only as far as the Kansas town of Wichita. Other trails forked off from the Chisholm Trail, leading to Abilene and other Kansas cattle towns.

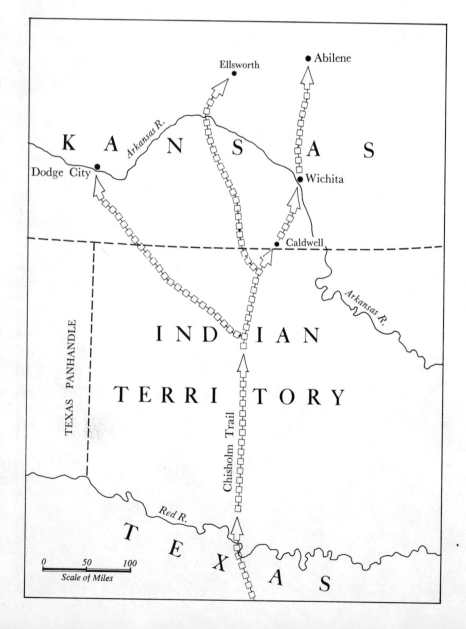

*The Chisholm Trail ran from Texas, through Indian territory into Kansas.*

*Jesse Chisholm,
who marked out the Chisholm
Trail, was part Cherokee.*
(OKLAHOMA HISTORICAL SOCIETY)

*Cattlemen attacked by Indians, an episode in the opening up of the
cattle country, by Frederic Remington.* (NEW YORK PUBLIC LIBRARY)

*Road branding before a trail drive.* (NEW YORK PUBLIC LIBRARY, RARE BOOK DIVISION)

After 1867, trail driving became more and more common. Sometimes an entire trail herd belonged to a single rancher. Other trail herds were made up of cattle belonging to several different small ranches. Still other ranchers sold their cattle to a drover after the roundup. The drover paid the rancher a certain price per head of cattle, then drove the cattle over the trail to the railhead market and tried to get a better price from the buyer there. The drover gave the cattle a new trail or road brand, so it could be proved that they all belonged to the same herd.

The cattle themselves were a mixture of breeds. In the early days of trail drives, the majority were tough, wiry Texas Longhorns. But other kinds of cattle were beginning to be raised, too. Hereford cattle, which had originally been brought to North America from England, were being raised in the southeast. Texas ranchers started to buy Hereford bulls and mate them with Longhorn cows. The result of this crossbreeding was a much heavier, meatier kind of cattle, which came to be known as "Whiteface." Whiteface cattle eventually became more important and more common than the Longhorns.

*A cowboy roping a Whiteface steer.*
(THE BETTMANN ARCHIVE)

*A trail drive gets underway.* (THE BETTMANN ARCHIVE)

Not all cattlemen agreed on the best way to begin a trail drive. Some believed in going very fast for the first few days of the drive, covering as much as twenty-five miles a day. The hard pace helped the cattle get accustomed to being driven. But there were other cattlemen who felt that a herd traveled better over the long run if it started out slowly. A hard drive at the beginning could exhaust some of the weaker cattle. Also, cattle that had been driven too hard often lost so much weight that they became hard to sell at the end of the drive.

Every morning, after the trail camp was broken, the cattle were allowed to proceed at their own will for two or three miles, grazing as they went. Then they were herded into a long line and driven forward for several miles at a faster, more regular pace, until they reached the next stream or waterhole. A scout always went ahead to find out how far it was to water. After the cattle had drunk their fill, they were allowed to rest during the midday hours, while the cowboys had a meal. Then the herd was driven on again as far as the night camp.

*Cattle crossing a stream.* (DENVER PUBLIC LIBRARY WESTERN COLLECTION)

*Cowboys enjoying the midday meal.* (THE BETTMANN ARCHIVE)

The average herd on a trail drive numbered 3,000 head, which meant that there would be about ten cowboys along. In addition there was always a cook and a horse wrangler. The job of the horse wrangler was to look after the horse herd, which Texas cowboys called by the Spanish word *remuda.* In the remuda there were usually at least three horses for each man on the drive. The rest of the cowboys looked down on the job of horse wrangler. Sometimes the horse wrangler was a very young cowboy. Often he was a Mexican or an Indian.

During the day the remuda was driven along on one side of the long line of cattle, while the cook drove the chuck wagon on the other side. At night the horses were allowed to graze, to sleep, and to wander on their own. But the horse wrangler had to make sure that none of them ran away. Indians were particularly good at this part of the job. They seemed to need little sleep, and they had a special knack for knowing how far away a horse had wandered. Centuries of life on the plains had made the Indians sensitive to sounds and night movements of which the cowboy was not even aware.

*In with the horse herd, by Frederic Remington.* (NEW YORK PUBLIC LIBRARY)

*One way to make an enemy of the cook is shown in Charles Russell's painting,* Bronco to Breakfast. (MONTANA HISTORICAL SOCIETY — MAC-KAY COLLECTION)

The cowboys looked down on the horse wrangler because he did not work with the cattle herd itself. On the other hand, they respected the cook, who did far more than just prepare the food. He made sure that there was always enough wood for the campfire. He was in charge of the medical supplies, and often knew a good deal about practical medicine. He was responsible for driving the chuck wagon, which was likely to be pulled by oxen rather than horses. Oxen were slow, but they were stronger than horses. Driving oxen was not an easy job, however. All in all, the cook had to be a man of many talents.

During a trail drive, the cowboy's day consisted of nothing but work, food, and sleep for weeks on end. The hardest work was keeping the stragglers moving at the back of the herd. Because it was such a dusty, tiring, unpleasant job, it was usually given to the least experienced cowboys. But all the men shared in turn the hardship of the night guard. Whatever the time of day or night, there were always a number of cowboys on guard.

*Getting ready to go on night guard.* (KANSAS STATE HISTORICAL SOCIETY, TOPEKA)

# Chapter 4:
# The Boom Towns
# of Kansas

At fifteen miles a day it took more than two months to travel the thousand miles of the Chisholm Trail. At the end of the drive, the cattle were herded into pens built near the railroad tracks, to await shipment to the North and East. Driving the cattle into the pens, which was known as "yarding," was the cowboys' final job. The men had done little but work for a long time. Now they wanted entertainment. Since they were not paid until the end of the drive, they had money to spend. The desires of the trail-weary cowboy had much to do with the shaping of the trail town community.

*Yarding a herd for shipment on the Kansas Pacific Railway.* (NEW YORK PUBLIC LIBRARY, RARE BOOK DIVISION)

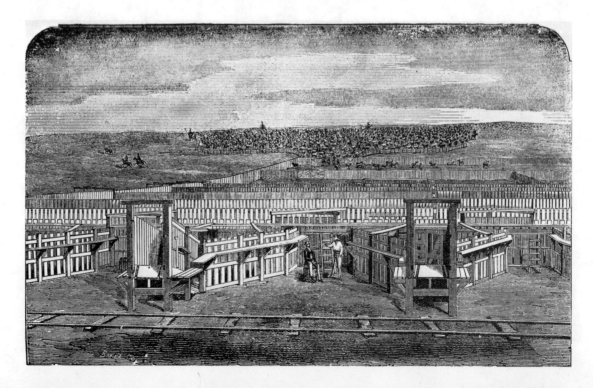

*Abilene in 1875, after the boom but still a cattle town.* (DENVER PUB-
LIC LIBRARY WESTERN COLLECTION)

Most of the trail towns sprang up practically overnight.
Hotels, saloons, dance halls, and even theaters were built
between one summer and the next. Abilene was the first
of these boom towns. It flourished for a while, and then
other towns, closer to Texas or easier to reach from the
trails, took its place. Abilene continued to be a less important cattle town for some years. Then it settled into a quiet
existence much like that of a thousand other towns
throughout the heartland of the country.

The next boom town after Abilene was Ellsworth, Kansas, which was easier to reach from the Chisholm Trail. To take advantage of this shift in the cattle trade, Joseph McCoy decided to move his hotel, called the Drover's Cottage. He dismantled it and moved parts of it from Abilene to Ellsworth on railroad boxcars. Throughout the 1870's and 1880's, still other towns became for a time the most important cattle-trading centers, one after another. Wichita, Dodge City, Caldwell, and Hays City were other Kansas towns that were to become part of the legend of the cowboy.

*Hays City, Kansas, in the 1870's.* (KANSAS STATE HISTORICAL SOCIETY)

*The Drover's Cottage in Abilene.* (KANSAS STATE HISTORICAL SOCIETY, TOPEKA)

*The Drover's Cottage in Ellsworth in 1872, after having been moved from Abilene.* (KANSAS HISTORICAL SOCIETY, TOPEKA)

*A group of cowboys going home to Texas from a cattle town.* (THE BETTMANN ARCHIVE)

Most of the business in the trail towns was done in the course of a very few months, in summer and early fall. Every room was taken in the hotels and boardinghouses. The restaurants, saloons, and dance halls did a huge business. But once the last of the cattle had been shipped out, everything changed. For the rest of the year, the towns were only half alive. There might be some building activity, as a new store, dance hall, or hotel went up. But most of the town's inhabitants were marking time until the first herd came lumbering in from Texas the following year.

*Wichita in 1873, the first year of its boom.* (KANSAS STATE HISTORICAL
SOCIETY, TOPEKA)

*Cowboys whooping it up in an Abilene Dance Hall.* (KANSAS STATE
HISTORICAL SOCIETY, TOPEKA)

# Chapter 5: Legendary Violence

The arrival of the trail herds each year meant money in the bank for the citizens of the boom town. But it could also mean problems. After the cowboys were paid, each man acted according to his individual nature. One man might peacefully buy a new set of clothes and have his picture taken at the local photographer's studio. But another might get involved in a violent brawl in a saloon, arguing over a woman or a gambling debt.

*Sometimes the cowboys were in such high spirits after reaching the end of the trail that they drove the herd right through the center of town, as here in Dodge City.* (NEW YORK PUBLIC LIBRARY)

*Arthur Walker
had his picture taken
in a photographer's studio.*
(DENVER PUBLIC LIBRARY
WESTERN COLLECTION)

*A barroom brawl.* (THE BETTMANN ARCHIVE)

59

Drunkenness and fighting sometimes led to killings in the Kansas boom towns. But the worst violence usually occurred when the towns were first being settled, before there was any local government. There were no railroads then, and no cattlemen. Later, during the great years of the cattle trade, between 1870 and 1880, local newspapers in the five most famous cattle towns — Abilene, Ellsworth, Wichita, Dodge City, and Caldwell — reported only about thirty killings altogether, spread out over ten years in the five different towns.

*A fight in the street, by Frederic Remington.* (NEW YORK PUBLIC LIBRARY)

*Drunken cowboys, by Frederic Remington.* (NEW YORK PUBLIC LIBRARY)

*Occasionally a group of cowboys would get drunk and start "hurrahing" a town, riding through the streets shooting their pistols into the air.* (NEW YORK PUBLIC LIBRARY)

Once they became well-established, the cattle towns brought their violence under control by passing laws and hiring marshals, sheriffs, and other law officers. Many of the marshals and sheriffs were famous men even before they were hired by the cattle towns. "Bear River Tom" Smith, the first marshal of Abilene, came from New York City, where he had broken up street gangs during the Civil War years. Of all the famous marshals of the Kansas cattle towns, he was the only one who was killed while serving as marshal. He was not killed by a cowboy, however, but by a local farmer.

*"Bear River Tom" Smith, marshal of Abilene.* (KANSAS STATE HISTORICAL SOCIETY, TOPEKA)

*Wild Bill Hickock wore his hair in ringlets and dressed in elegant clothes, but his ability with a gun kept other men from laughing at his vanity.* (KANSAS STATE HISTORICAL SOCIETY, TOPEKA)

Other marshals were hired because of their fame with a gun. The fact that a man had killed other men did not necessarily make him a criminal in the eyes of frontier communities. In many cases a man had to kill or be killed. Unless he was known to be a thief or a troublemaker, people often assumed that a man had no choice but to shoot. A marshal like Wild Bill Hickock made other men think twice about causing trouble. Wild Bill had been a buffalo hunter and he was extraordinarily good with a gun. He was marshal of Abilene in the early 1870's; later he was marshal of Hays City.

*Dodge City in April of 1879, before the start of its biggest season. Half a million cattle were shipped through the boom town in that year.* (KANSAS STATE HISTORICAL SOCIETY, TOPEKA)

Many of the violent stories of the trail driving era were told about Dodge City. It was the most important cattle town for a longer period than any of its rivals. Hundreds of thousands of cattle poured into Dodge City each season during the late 1870's. To keep order in the booming community, such figures as William B. ("Bat") Masterson and Wyatt Earp were hired as law officers. Both men had been involved in famous gunfighting incidents at various points in their lives. But there is no record of Bat Masterson having killed anyone in all the years he spent around Dodge City. Wyatt Earp may have killed one man.

*The Dodge City Peace Commission. Back row, left to right: W. Harris, Luke Short, Bat Masterson, W. F. Petillon. Front row, left to right: Charles Bassett, Wyatt Earp, M. F. McClain, Neal Brown.* (KANSAS STATE HISTORICAL SOCIETY,TOPEKA)

*"The Varieties," a Dodge City dance hall, photographed in 1878. Bat Masterson's brother George is tending bar.* (KANSAS STATE HISTORICAL (KANSAS STATE HISTORICAL SOCIETY, TOPEKA)

*The Long Branch Saloon.* (KANSAS STATE HISTORICAL SOCIETY, TOPEKA)

The trail town law officers were paid very little, in spite of their fame. Most of them supplemented their incomes in other ways. Luke Short, for instance, ran the gambling tables at Dodge City's famous Long Branch Saloon. It was there that another famous gunfighter, John ("Doc") Halliday, a dentist turned gambler, saved Wyatt Earp's life in 1878 when Earp was threatened by a gang of rustlers. Such true incidents, and many more fictional ones, have been portrayed over and over again in twentieth-century novels, films, and television shows.

The more that people in the East heard about the West, the more they wanted to hear. Writers and artists traveled widely in the West, searching for subject matter. Frederic Remington's superb drawings of the West and its people appeared regularly in the famous *Century Magazine*. Some of his best cowboy drawings illustrated a series of articles by a future President of the United States, Theodore Roosevelt. Another fine artist, Charles M. Russell, worked for several years as a cowboy before he married and devoted full time to his painting.

*Charles M. Russell
as a young man,
in a cowboy outfit.*
(THE BETTMANN ARCHIVE)

There were other journalists and artists, however, who were more interested in excitement than in the truth. The drawing on this page is a typical exaggeration of the time. The cowboys are pictured not just "hurrahing" a town, but actually taking it over. The caption that accompanied the picture when it was originally published stated that two out of three cowboys spent their off duty hours robbing the stores of the nearest town. That kind of story was pure fiction, but it sold newspapers in the eastern states.

*An exaggerated picture of cowboys robbing a town.* (THE BETTMANN ARCHIVE)

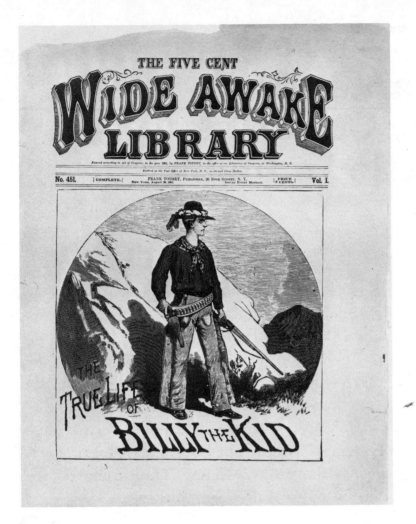

*The Wide Awake Library edition of* The True Life of Billy the Kid, *published a few weeks after his death.* (YALE UNIVERSITY LIBRARY — COE COLLECTION)

There were probably more stories written about Billy the Kid, both before and after his death, than about any other figure of the great days of the cattle trade. Yet, he worked as a cowboy for only a brief period at the end of his short life. Billy's real name was William H. Bonney. According to legend, he killed his first man when he was twelve, because the man had insulted his mother. He killed another twenty before he died at the age of twenty-one. A few weeks after his death, the first of many books about Billy the Kid was on sale in the East, and another legend was born.

69

# Chapter 6:
# The Changing
# Cattle Industry

While the legends about the West were growing, the beef industry that had created them was both growing and changing. By 1877, when Dodge City was the great cattle-shipping town, 500,000 head were passing through it each season. Great fortunes were being made raising beef cattle. Those fortunes were the subject of a book called *The Beef Bonanza or How to Get Rich on the Plains,* written by a man named James Brisbin. The book inspired many more men to go into the cattle business. The raising of beef cattle became a major American industry.

*Cattle being killed in a packinghouse in Kansas City.* (NEW YORK PUBLIC LIBRARY, RARE BOOK DIVISION)

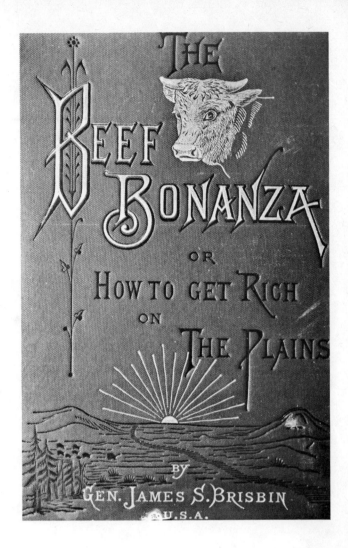

The cover of James Brisbin's
book on the beef industry.
(FROM Trail Driving Days,
COURTESY OF THE AUTHORS,
DEE BROWN AND MARTIN F. SCHMITT)

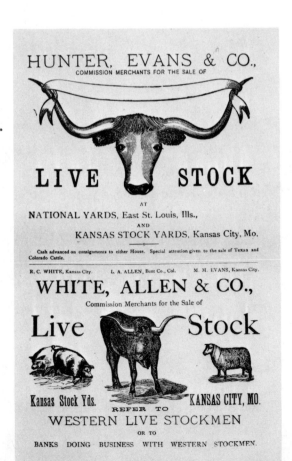

Advertisement for
cattle agents from
the back pages of Joseph McCoy's
Historic Sketches
of the Cattle Trade.
(NEW YORK PUBLIC
LIBRARY, RARE
BOOK DIVISION)

71

*The main house of the King Ranch in the late nineteenth century.*
(NEW YORK PUBLIC LIBRARY)

Some of the ranches in the Southwest grew so large that they were referred to as "cattle empires." One of the most famous was the King Ranch, which got its start before the Civil War. In the 1850's, Richard King began raising cattle for their hides on the coastal plain of Texas. A few years later he took on as a ranching partner a man named Mifflin Kennedy. After the war, in 1868, King and Kennedy divided the ranch between them, each taking 150,000 acres. Then, as trail driving opened a great new market, Richard King's ranch began to grow again, until it covered more than 500,000 acres.

An important factor in the growth of the cattle trade was the slaughter of the American buffalo for their valuable hides. Between 1870 and 1875, almost four million of them had been killed in the Southwest alone, and the species was almost extinct. The Indians had hunted the buffalo for food and clothing, and many of their religious ceremonies were inspired by the buffalo. After the white men killed these animals off, the Indians gave up the battle for their lands and retired to the reservations set aside for them by the United States government. The grassy plains and cattle trails were left to the ranchers.

*The way of life of the Plains Indians was based on the buffalo hunt. By destroying the buffalo, the white man destroyed the Indians' way of life.* (SMITHSONIAN INSTITUTION)

The beef industry was growing, but it was also changing. In 1881 a new kind of cattle car with individual stalls was introduced by the railroads. By the 1880's another invention, barbed wire, was having a great effect on cattle ranching. No longer did cattle roam freely on the great ranges. The land was divided up, with the boundaries marked by barbed wire. Many ranchers began to grow hay to feed their cattle in winter. And the association roundup ceased to exist, because each rancher's cattle grazed entirely on his own land.

*A cowboy checking the line of the barbed wire fence, by Frederic Remington.* (THE BETTMANN ARCHIVE)

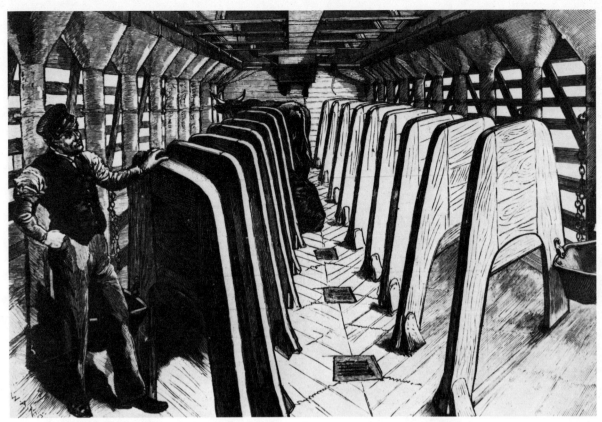

*A new kind of cattle car, with individual stalls, was introduced in
1881.* (THE BETTMANN ARCHIVE)

*Hay being gathered for winter feeding on a Nevada ranch.* (NEW
YORK PUBLIC LIBRARY)

*Cattle being herded across a Montana river.* (DENVER PUBLIC LIBRARY WESTERN COLLECTION)

More and more ranchers, and farmers as well, settled in the Southwest. More and more barbed wire went up. Cattlemen began looking for new open ranges on which to raise their cattle. In the Northwest there were still great open grasslands, free ranges as yet unsettled. Big Texas ranches such as the XIT and the Matador also established themselves in the Northwest. Cattle ranching continued to be of great importance in Texas, too. But by the mid-1880's, the place to make a quick "bonanza" fortune was in the northwest.

The changes continued. The northern climate required a different cowboy costume. When he went range riding in winter, the cowboy wore fur-covered chaps on his legs, a heavy coat, a fur hat, and thick gloves. Now there were no more thousand-mile cattle drives. The railroad was spreading rapidly into every corner of the country, and the distance to the nearest shipping pens grew shorter and shorter. Meat packing plants were built much closer to the great ranches, and fewer live cattle were shipped to the East.

*A northwestern cowboy riding the range in winter.* (NEW YORK PUBLIC LIBRARY)

The kind of man who owned the ranches on which the cowboys worked was changing, too. A large ranch in the Dakotas was built in the 1880's by a French nobleman, the Marquis de Mores. Nearby, a future president of the United States, Theodore Roosevelt, was running two ranches and writing some of the articles on the West that were published in *Century Magazine*. In Cheyenne, Wyoming, wealthy cattlemen belonged to the imposing Cheyenne Club. Many ranch owners now were Eastern businessmen whose ranches were just one of many investments.

*The Cheyenne Club, seen here during the 1880's, was far more elegant than the famous Drover's Cottage of Abilene and Ellsworth had been ten years earlier.* (WYOMING STATE ARCHIVES AND HISTORICAL DEPARTMENT)

*Herd of Montana cattle threatened by a blizzard.* (THE BETTMANN
ARCHIVE)

In January of 1887 the American Northwest was struck by
the Great Blizzard. It howled for three days across the
ranges, depositing snow as high as a cowboy's shoulders.
Range cattle died by the hundreds of thousands. At
roundup time the following spring, only a few miserable
survivors of the great range herds could be found. Rancher
after rancher went bankrupt. The great herds had been
driven north from the open ranges of Texas by barbed wire
and the increasing population. Now nature herself had
spoken the final word. The days of open-range ranching
were gone forever.

79

# Chapter 7:
# The End of an Era

An entire era was drawing to a close. The spreading railroads, the new refrigerated railway cars, and the increasing number of packing plants had put an end to trail driving. The Kansas trail towns settled down to the routine of a thousand other communities. There were still ranches and there were still cowboys. But they were just one part of a vast, well-regulated business enterprise linking the western ranches with the huge stockyards of Chicago. The open ranges, the trail drives, and the Kansas boom towns were all fading into history.

*The Chicago Stockyards in 1893.* (THE BETTMANN ARCHIVE)

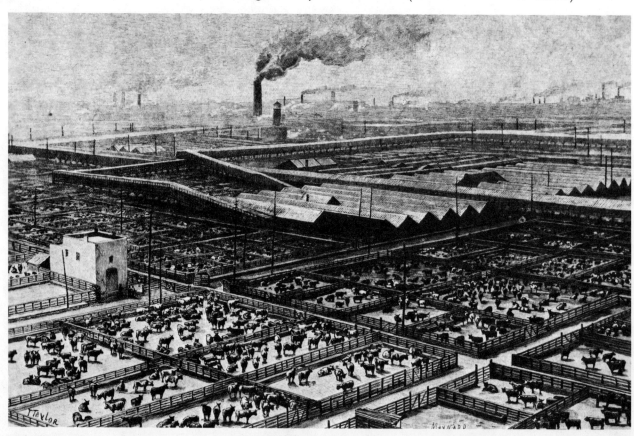

*A photograph of Nat Love from his book* The Life and Adventures of Nat Love.
(THE WILLIAM LOREN KATZ COLLECTION)

Although the West itself was changing, the public appetite for stories about it steadily increased. From the 1890's well into the twentieth century, one cowboy after another wrote down the story of his youthful adventures on the ranches and trails of the old West. James H. Cook described what it was like to be attacked by Sioux Indians on a cattle drive from Texas to the Dakotas. Nat Love wrote a colorful and somewhat exaggerated account of his life as "Deadwood Dick." Andy Adams, W. S. James, and Charlie Siringo wrote classic accounts of the days of the great trail drives.

81

Even more popular with the public than books about the old West were various kinds of theatrical presentations. One of the earliest was the Dodge City Cowboy Band, which marched in the inaugural parade of President Benjamin Harrison in 1889. Buffalo Bill Cody, who had hunted along with Wild Bill Hickock, mounted a Wild West Show. Buffalo Bill made much of his friendship with such figures as Hickock and Sitting Bull, the last of the great Sioux Indian chiefs. And, finally, the commercial rodeo show was born, in which cowboys roped steers and rode bucking broncos for a paying audience.

*The Dodge City Cowboy Band.* (DENVER PUBLIC LIBRARY WESTERN COLLECTION)

*Buffalo Bill Cody
photographed with
Sitting Bull.*
(DENVER PUBLIC LIBRARY
WESTERN COLLECTION)

*Bill Pickett,
an early rodeo star,
on his horse Spradley.*
(UNIVERSITY OF OKLAHOMA,
WESTERN HISTORY
COLLECTIONS, LIBRARY)

# Conclusion

The cowboy legend grew out of a particular period of history and a special set of circumstances. The great open ranges, the thousand-mile trail drives, and the booming Kansas cattle towns created a way of life as colorful as any in American history. That way of life flourished for less than twenty-five years. It was made possible not only by the great open spaces of the Western frontier, but also by the march of progress. Without railroads and packing plants, there would have been no beef bonanza. The march of progress continued, and eventually it destroyed the way of life that it had helped make possible. But the names of the places and the men of that time would not be forgotten, nor would the legendary stories about them.

*A cowboy on
horseback,
by Frederic Remington.*
(NEW YORK PUBLIC
LIBRARY)

# Glossary

ASSOCIATION — a group of ranchers who grazed their cattle on the same open range land.

BRAND — a mark — sometimes in the form of initials, sometimes a design — put on cattle and horses to identify ownership. Branding is done by applying a heated iron rod to the hide of the animal.

BRONCO — Spanish word meaning wild horse.

CHAPS — protective leather pieces worn over trousers. In the Northwest, they were often covered with fur for extra warmth.

CHUCK WAGON — covered wagon, usually drawn by oxen, containing the food and utensils used by the cook to prepare meals for the cowboys out on the range or on a trail drive.

CORRAL — a wooden or rope enclosure in which horses and cattle are kept, originally a Spanish word.

CUTTING OUT — the job of separating one animal from the rest of the herd so that it can be roped.

DROVER — a man who drives cattle on the trail.

HEAD — term used in counting cattle and horses. One head is one animal. A thousand head is a thousand animals.

HIDE — the outer skin of an animal.

JAYHAWKERS — slang name for the Kansas farmers who prevented Texas cattle from crossing their lands.

LASSO — the rope used by the cowboy to capture animals that are running free, originally a Spanish word.

LONGHORN — the kind of cattle brought from Spain by early explorers. Centuries later the descendants of the original Spanish cattle became the foundation of the American beef industry.

MARSHAL — law officer in the western towns.

RAILHEAD — the furthest point to which the railroad track had been laid, as the railroads spread westward.

REMUDA — Spanish word for the horse herd.

RODEO — a contest or show in which cowboys perform tricks of riding and roping.

RUSTLERS — cattle thieves.

SOMBRERO — the large, broad-brimmed hat popular in Mexico taken over by the American cowboy. The American version was called a *stetson*.

SPURS — sharp metal prongs worn on cowboy boots to help the men control their horses.

WHITEFACE — a kind of cattle, originally from northern Europe, that became important in the later development of the beef industry.

YARDING — driving a herd of cattle into pens by the railroad tracks.

# Index

MCCOY, JOSEPH, 40, 54
Marshals, 62-69
Masterson, William B. (Bat), 64
Mexico, cowboys in, 3
Mores, Marquis de, 78
Mustangs. *See* Horses, wild.

ONE Horse Charley, 8

PACKING houses, 1, 6, 38, 84

RAILROADS, 1, 38, 40, 44, 52, 54, 74, 80, 84
Ranches, ranching, 3-8, 10-37, 71-79. *See also* Trail drivers.
Range land, 10, 28
Remington, Frederic, 67
Remuda, 48, 49
Rodeos, 82
Roosevelt, Theodore, 67, 78
Roundup, 10-11, 22, 37, 74
Russell, Charles M., 67
Rustlers, 15, 27

SCOUTS, 47
Sedalia, 38-40
Sheriffs. *See* Marshals.
Short, Luke, 66
Siringo, Charlie, 81
Sitting Bull, 82
Smith, Bear River Tom, 62
Sombreros, 32
Spurs, 31
Stampedes, 22-27, 38
Stetson hats, 32

TRAIL drives, 30, 34, 37, 38-51, 84

VAQUEROS, 3

WHITEFACE cattle, 45
Wichita, 42. *See also* Boom towns.
Wranglers, 48, 50

YARDING, 52

89

## ABOUT THE AUTHOR

John Malone grew up on the campus of Phillips Academy, Andover, where his father taught American history for twenty-five years. He was nineteen when his first short story was accepted for publication. Having attended Harvard College, Mr. Malone went to Europe, where he remained for four years, living in Paris, Rome, London, and Spain. In 1965, he returned to New York City, where he has lived ever since, working as a free-lance writer and editor.